FAMILY CLUSTER PROGRAMS

Resources for Intergenerational Bible Study

R. Ted Nutting

FAMILY CLUSTER PROGRAMS

Resources for Intergenerational Bible Study

R. Ted Nutting

FAMILY CLUSTER PROGRAMS

Library of Congress Cataloging in Publication Data

Nutting, R   Ted.
    Family cluster programs.

    Bibliography: p. 77.
    1. Family—Religious life.   2. Jesus Christ
—Parables—Study.   I.   Title.
BV4526.2N87   268'.6   77-20188
ISBN 0-8170-0776-8

The name JUDSON PRESS is registered as a trademark in the U.S. Patent Office.
Printed in the U.S.A. ⊕

The preparation of this material has been an education in itself. It reflects refinements suggested by users of the sessions from the First Christian Church in Loveland, Colorado, and Broadway Baptist Church in Denver, Colorado.

Indirect credit must be given to families from four Loveland churches who suggested I prepare the material as a result of an ecumenical family cluster experiment. The churches involved were the First Baptist Church (where I serve as Minister of Christian Growth), Mountain View United Presbyterian Church, First United Methodist Church, and the First Christian Church (Disciples of Christ).

I am especially grateful to the Reverend Joe Leonard, Director of Family Life Education for the American Baptist Churches, U.S.A., for his encouragement to develop the material in book form. He has provided personal counsel which has helped simplify the writing.

My real source of knowledge about family life is my own experience with my wife, Kitty, and my son, Donnie. They are the immediate channel of God's grace that keeps me motivated to finish what I begin. Also included in my family are my own parents, Clifford and Ethel Nutting, who have encouraged me to write since my high school years.

I pray the influence of all these people, through this book, will enrich the families who use it.

R. Ted Nutting

Contents

Introduction

We hear much about family cluster education these days, and many people are experimenting with it. However, planned units for such learning experiences are scarce. This book is written for those who have little background in developing sessions that fit the needs of the family but who want to give family cluster education a try. It contains a unit of study and fun designed specifically for family cluster education in the church.

A WORD ABOUT FAMILY CLUSTER

Although this unit is designed with the traditional family in mind, it may be adapted to other kinds of "family" groups which make up a household. Such groups may include a single person (unmarried, widowed, or divorced), a couple with or without children, a single parent with children, three- or four-generation families, or any other combination.

Family cluster education is a design of learning that keeps the members of such a family unit together most of the time in learning experiences with other family groups. The term was first used by Dr.

Margaret Sawin in the First Baptist Church of Rochester, New York. Many other churches have experimented with it and have adapted the concept to fit their own needs. It is best fitted to those who place a high value on sharing some of the more important learnings of life with other members of their family who are of different ages. It will succeed most with those adults who feel free to communicate with children on their level and with children and teenagers who are willing to try to understand adults on their level. Some of us have to be freed from our inhibitions as adults to play with our children in front of other adults for fear we will look silly. In our culture this seems to be more true of fathers than mothers. But we can be freed from those inhibitions, and the liberation is redemptive.

HOW TO RECRUIT PARTICIPANTS

This family cluster material is not meant to be therapeutic in nature but educational. It is important for those you recruit to understand that you will not be dealing with deep family problems that really should be handled in a counseling situation.

I suggest that you begin with well-adjusted families which you feel would be interested in this type of experience. Give them a brief but specific outline of what to expect and obtain a clear commitment from each member of the family to participate. It is important for all members of the family to take part together.

HOW TO BEGIN

Plan a retreat: One excellent way to get started is to plan a retreat. This can be costly for families unless subsidized by the church, especially if it is held in the winter when winterized lodges are needed. However, a little searching will turn up the right place. Summer family camping is an ideal way to plan such a retreat because it can be done economically.

The outdoor setting provides many opportunities for learning experiences. An outline of a retreat program is included in the Appendix. The book by John D. Rozeboom, *Family Camping—Five Designs for Your Church,*[1] has some excellent ideas for this kind of family cluster retreat.

[1] John D. Rozeboom, *Family Camping—Five Designs for Your Church* (Nashville: Board of Discipleship of The United Methodist Church, 1973).

The retreat should be planned so there is a mixture of family recreation and learning experiences, not necessarily related to the unit you plan to use. It is helpful to plan for some recreation for the children, teenagers, and adults separately from each other. It would also be good to provide a block of time in which individual families can participate in an activity alone. Too much "togetherness" may overburden the learning experiences you have together. It is best to bring in someone experienced with family cluster education for your retreat so that it can be a training session for your leaders as well as for all the participants. Much can be done in a weekend retreat toward training and building relationships. Much more intimacy and trust can be established with longer retreats. One weekend is better than none at all and often is the key to success in the following weeks. Don't overlook the possibility of having a "lock in" type retreat in your church. The classrooms can be used for sleeping quarters, and other rooms in the building for learning experiences. "Lock ins" are good in the wintertime when it is too expensive to take families to lodges.

Contracting: Sometime during the retreat the adults and teenagers should get together for "contracting." This can be a time-consuming process; so it may be best to plan other activities for the small children during this time. "Contracting" is another term for working out agreements on when to meet, where, how frequently, whether or not to meet with a meal first followed by learning experiences, and so on. This should be done at the retreat. A skilled leader at the retreat can offer suggestions on the various types of meetings that can be planned. Some examples include meeting on Saturday afternoons and closing with a meal as a love feast, a weeknight meeting for a meal followed by learning activities, Sunday morning in place of the regular church school time, Sunday afternoon or evening meetings, or any combination which you happen to think of. Don't be surprised at the struggle of the group as it makes these decisions. It is often hard for a new group to arrive at a consensus on schedules. Everyone has an objection to each suggestion, but don't let that discourage you. By the time they have had a good retreat together, they have a great deal of motivation to solve such problems. I see these struggles as the essential birth pangs of a new group. There is no need to feel discouraged over the difficulty of the group to arrive at a decision. You can get the ball rolling by offering suggestions or alternatives, then summarizing what you hear the group saying. After a few minutes of discussion you will recognize one idea getting more favorable attention than others. Reflect this to the group to let participants know what you hear emerging. That will speed them on their way. Once one idea seems to have good support, summarize and get definite commitments from all members of the group. When they have reached that point, they have made a group decision.

There should be a clear understanding among all participants that everyone is expected to *try* a suggested activity. However, if the activity just does not fit them, they should feel free to move in and out of learning experiences without the rest of the group feeling embarrassed or insulted. This is especially true for younger children. There should also be an understood commitment by each one to pray for the other members of the group daily.

HOW PEOPLE LEARN

It is important to mix learning experiences among three basic groupings. Use a minimum of activities which are of the "telling" nature, such as story telling, listening to records, or lecturing. Use more activities that require the visual attention of the participants, such as filmstrips, skits, films, or object lessons. *Maximize* the use of activities requiring the participants to do something themselves that is related to the theme, such as making collages, putting on a skit they have created, paraphrasing the story and acting it out, or reflecting on experiences they have had similar to the topic they are discussing.

The "cone of learning" (Figure 1) illustrates why active types of learning experiences are more effective, though they should not be used exclusively.

Another important factor in learning is that people learn things at different levels. Charles and Dorothy Christine, in *Practical Guide to Curriculum and Instruction,* identify four levels of learning which one passes through before the lesson becomes part of his or her life pattern. These are: (1) familiarity, (2) knowledge, (3) understanding, and (4) application.[2] If you have looked up the locations of the

[2] Charles T. and Dorothy W. Christine, *Practical Guide to Curriculum and Instruction* (Englewood Cliffs, N. J.: Prentice-Hall, Inc., 1971), p. 19.

parables in the Bible and have read them, but that is all, you have a *familiarity* with them. If you study the background material in the study unit and other resources so you know what the parable is about and why Jesus used it, you will have a *knowledge* of the parables. If you begin looking for experiences in your own life that are similar to those talked about in the parables, you are at the level of

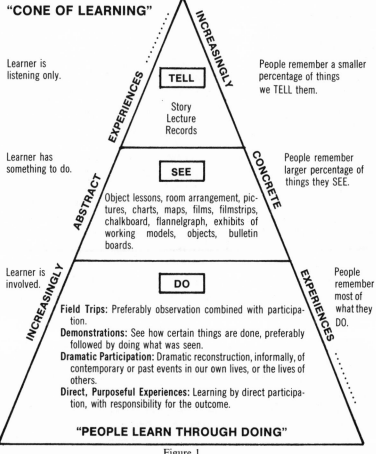

"CONE OF LEARNING"

Learner is listening only.

INCREASINGLY

EXPERIENCES

TELL

Story
Lecture
Records

People remember a smaller percentage of things we TELL them.

Learner has something to do.

ABSTRACT

CONCRETE

SEE

Object lessons, room arrangement, pictures, charts, maps, films, filmstrips, chalkboard, flannelgraph, exhibits of working models, objects, bulletin boards.

People remember larger percentage of things they SEE.

Learner is involved.

INCREASINGLY

EXPERIENCES

DO

Field Trips: Preferably observation combined with participation.

Demonstrations: See how certain things are done, preferably followed by doing what was seen.

Dramatic Participation: Dramatic reconstruction, informally, of contemporary or past events in our own lives, or the lives of others.

Direct, Purposeful Experiences: Learning by direct participation, with responsibility for the outcome.

People remember most of what they DO.

"PEOPLE LEARN THROUGH DOING"

Figure 1

Adapted from Mildred Arnold, "How Children Learn" (unpublished), and Edgar Dale, *Audio-Visual Methods in Teaching* (New York: Dryden Press, 1946), p. 38.

understanding. When the lesson of the parable begins to affect the decisions you make from day to day, you have reached the *application* level. All levels should be covered, but they can be approached in different ways and in any sequence.

Application of the lesson is the ultimate goal, but you get there best by covering the other three levels. It is important to try to know where participants might be in regard to a given lesson. Application may not really occur until several weeks after the session.

HOW TO USE THIS UNIT

One leader versus rotated leadership: Rotating leadership from session to session adds variety and sometimes increases ownership of the program if each leader feels confident to carry that role. If this is the group's first experience with family cluster, it may be best to have one leader who participates as an individual without his or her family present. This way the leader is free to observe and move in and out of activities with the participants. However, even a single leader should adjust the sessions and learning activities according to feedback sought and received from the participants.

Planning the sessions: If the members of your group are basically passive and comfortable with letting the leader make the plans, that process may work best. However, if they like lots of input in the planning, it should be done with them at special meetings other than the regular sessions.

I feel it is best to find some way to get input from a cross section of the group so all ages and interests are represented as much as possible. Too few involved in planning increases chances of missing the interests and needs of the group. Too many involved in planning causes the process to bog down with too many minor conflicts and differences. Each group needs to discover its own way of functioning. One quite safe way to go about it is to have the main leader give more direction in the earlier sessions, gradually increasing the involvement of others in the planning and leadership of the later sessions. By the end of six sessions others will probably feel more comfortable in the leadership role and will express their ideas more readily. Experience has an amazing way of creating new ideas and motivation in people who initially do not know which direction to go.

The learning objective: The objective or learning goal of each session should be stated in easily measurable terms and should take into consideration the learning level of the participants with regard to the material in the session being planned. A good book for help in preparing instructional objectives is *Preparing Instructional Objectives* by Robert F. Mager (Belmont, Calif.: Fearon Publishers, Inc., 1962). The basic plans in this unit are for giving you a start. You should adapt them to your own needs.

Use of resources: Some resources are suggested at the end of each session. Others are listed in the Appendix. More are listed than you will ever use, especially films and filmstrips. In planning, be sure to plan far enough ahead to give time for securing the resources you plan to use. Vary the type of resources and experiences from session to session to help keep up interest and motivation. Also, don't always plan everything on the level of a child's understanding. Some sessions should be geared toward adults and others toward teenagers.

The most important thing to do in using resources is to utilize your own ideas and people in your group or your church. Use outside resources, such as films and filmstrips, only occasionally, and then only because they get the point across better than anything you can come up with. Don't stifle your own creativity. You will be surprised at the resources and ideas you discover in your own group.

In the case of some of the records, the same material is available in book form and can be read aloud. Those are indicated in the resource listings after each session.

The records, films, and filmstrips suggested are available for purchase, rent, or loan either from the publisher or from denominational libraries, local ecumenical resource centers, local visual aid centers in larger metropolitan areas, or perhaps from local churches. Quite often, if your denominational library does not have the resource you need, you may find a library from another denomination represented in your town that has it.

Planning alternatives: It is helpful to plan a few alternate activities for children if they become disinterested in a particular learning experience. However, the alternate activity should not distract them from the main program. Avoid meeting where there are items of furniture or other objects that are hazardous to children and will consequently cause parents to be anxious and distracted from the learning experience. The meeting area needs to be large enough to accommodate these activities in the same room so that children can drop out when the going gets rough, yet be close enough to the action so they can rejoin the group easily.

EVALUATION OF THE INDIVIDUAL SESSIONS

The key to good evaluation of a session is a clearly stated learning goal or objective, prepared in such a way that it can be measured. If you achieved your goal with little effort, you may have aimed too low. If you fell short, it may have been an unrealistic goal or you may not have planned learning activities that related clearly to the goal. If you achieved it with some challenging effort, pat yourself on the back. You probably had an exciting session.

Some evaluation can be done at the end of each session, but it should be planned so that it is part of the total experience and flows naturally from it. Such questions as, "What new thing did you learn about yourself?" or "What did you like best about this session?" or "What did you enjoy doing most?" can be asked during a closure or worship time. Use positive questions to evoke affirmative responses from the participants. However, if there are some negative reactions to be heard, the leader should find time with the participants or representatives to delve a little deeper. Evaluation should always call for positive suggestions for future sessions and activities or it leaves the leader without direction. It is the responsibility of each participant to offer his or her positive suggestions.

SOME IDEAS ABOUT PARABLES

Jesus taught in parables to help people understand the deeper truth of what he was talking about. With deeper understanding they could make a better application to their own lives. The parables were stories based on the experiences of Jesus' listeners.

People today have experiences that are similar to those of people in Jesus' day, but in different contexts. Therefore the parables have to be retold and adapted to new situations. However, the message that Jesus was conveying by use of the parable is unchanged because it is one of eternal truth, much like the messages found in fables or other nonreligious literature of past centuries.

The purpose of this unit is to discover how the message Jesus was teaching through the parables can be applied to experiences of modern families. The person leading the sessions in the unit should try to draw from families' experiences that are similiar to the parables which Jesus used.

What Is a Parable?

It has been said that a parable is "an earthly story with a heavenly meaning." To be more correct, we should have to say it is an earthly story with *just one* heavenly meaning. A common mistake in interpreting the parables is to treat them as allegories. Allegories often have several different meanings, with each part of the story having some parallel to each facet of truth with which it deals. With only one or two exceptions, the parables are told to express only one very simple and pointed truth.

Each session in this unit will have a paragraph listing the one basic meaning of the parable under the title **THE HEAVENLY MEANING,** referring to its one *eternal truth.* Following that will be a paragraph under the title **THE EARTHLY STORY,** referring to the background of the story in Jesus' day and modern examples in our day for children, teenagers, adults, and families. **THE LEARNING GOAL** will indicate a simple goal or objective for the session. Some **POSSIBLE LEARNING ACTIVITIES** will be listed with suggested resources which should help the participants reach the goal. These activities are arranged in alternate plans. Don't expect to use all the activities suggested. Choose those that will match the needs of your group and provide a variety of experiences. You may even wish to use activities from both alternate plans in one session.

A basic thesis of this unit is that the Bible is more effective if the learners can see how it fits their own experiences. When such a match is made, the Bible brings great spiritual enrichment to the learners.

Session I.
The Parable of the
Lost Sheep

THE HEAVENLY MEANING

It is not the will of our Father that one of these little ones should perish. God cares for those whom other people regard as unimportant. He loves each person. One person lost in the crowd is important to God. We are important to him because he has created each one of us in his image to be special persons.

THE EARTHLY STORY

In Jesus' Day

Because of the ruggedness of the country around Judea it was easy for a sheep to get away from the herd and become trapped on a dangerous ledge. It was often necessary for the shepherd to rescue such strays at great risk to himself. Because of the limited herds, each animal was very important to the shepherd.

In Our Day

For children: Many children have experienced the fear and panic of getting lost from their parents in a shopping center or in a crowd of people. They can identify with the fear, followed by the relief and joy of being found. Some children have also been given ideas of God that are frightening to them. This parable says that God loves "the little ones." It is a beautiful, positive message for children.

For teenagers: Teenagers are often struggling with finding their own importance in life. "Does anyone really care?" "Does anybody really love me?" "Do my ideas count at all in the decisions my family makes?" This parable says "yes" to all those questions.

For adults: Adults sometimes feel lost in the world when they feel the weight of family responsibilities or the trauma of a change in jobs or careers. In an automated society they often feel displaced by the machine. This parable says they count in God's world; they are significant. However, they need help in knowing exactly how they count or in what ways they are significant. They also know the feeling of anxiety when their children are lost or in danger. They can gain an understanding from their feelings of how God feels about us when we are groping for a direction in life.

For families: The family can provide the ideal setting where every member belongs. Other family members should be concerned and involved when one member is experiencing some form of "lostness."

POSSIBLE LEARNING ACTIVITIES
Getting Started

In each session the "getting started" activities are to introduce the theme and to get people interested in it quickly.

Alternate 1	*Alternate 2*
1. Plan ahead of time for someone to "lose" a trinket or object of which he or she is very fond by having someone else hide it for him or her. Let the person look for it until he or she finds it, taking long enough for others also to start looking. After the object has been found, read the parable from the Bible (Matthew 18:1-14); then break up into	**1.** Arrange ahead of time for a few people to do a skit reenacting what it means to be lost. The skit need be only about five minutes long. The plot could be a modern one in which some person gets lost in the crowd, the crowd being all the other participants. One person is the searcher, looking for the lost person. Participants can act it

smaller groups to continue the session.

Developing the Session

Alternate 1

1. Break up into small groups of two or three families each. Discuss briefly the meaning of the story. The adults can listen to the children telling of experiences when they were lost and how they felt when they were found. Or each one could share how he or she felt when a lost object which meant very much to them was found.

2. After the participants have discussed the parable enough to show that they have an understanding of the lesson, ask them to rewrite the parable in a contemporary setting. If they seem to have difficulty getting the idea, the leader should make suggestions drawing from the introductory material at the beginning of this session.

3. Have each family plan an action project in which they choose someone they know who seems "lost" in some way and needs to be "found." Encourage them to think of specific ways to "find" their friends.

out nonverbally or improvise their own script as they role-play the situation.

Alternate 2

1. Break up into small groups as in Alternate 1. Discuss the meaning of the story and have the participants share similar experiences of their own when they felt lost and were found. Provide newspapers and magazines for the participants to use in making a collage. Ask them to find pictures or captions showing "lostness" or examples of someone caring or of someone being "found." Have them glue the cutout pictures to a large sheet of newsprint. Parents will find the activity helpful in stimulating discussion in their family as they help their children identify feelings. Encourage parents to listen for feelings their children are expressing by listing all they heard when the collage is finished.

2. Have the groups share the feelings the collage making evoked. Then have them identify individuals or groups in their community who are "lost" and discuss ways in which they might be "found" with their help.

Examples of lost people: Lonely senior citizens who have gifts that are not being used; youth who have many "dreamy" ideas, but no one seems to want to listen; people who are poor and do not know how to help themselves; people who are rich, but find no meaning in their wealth; bereaved persons who are bitter but need someone to talk to who can say by action, "I care about you."

Concluding the Session

In this part of each session two things need to be accomplished. One is to review the things that have been learned from the activities. The other is to celebrate in a worship fashion what has been learned and commitments that have been made.

Alternate 1

1. Ask persons from the group to share their contemporary parable with the total group.

2. Ask those who are willing to express a sense in which they feel lost. Instruct the total group to respond in litany fashion to each person who shares by saying, "We believe in you in Jesus' name."

3. Ask the group members to mingle and tell one or two other people some good quality or gift they see in the other person.

4. Sing "His Sheep Am I" or some other song dealing with the theme.

5. Close with prayer, asking God to help each person know that he or she is loved by God and asking him to help them encourage others who are lost.

Alternate 2

1. Ask each family or group to share its collage and describe or interpret it to the rest of the group.

2. Ask each family or group to share its project for the next week without giving names of people whom they intend to help.

3. Sing "Amazing Grace" or some other song dealing with the theme.

4. Close with a litany. Either use the one found at the end of this session or have the group make up its own.

Use your imagination in celebration. Keep it relevant to the theme. Respect each person's freedom to participate or not participate.

SUGGESTED RESOURCES FOR THIS SESSION

For a more complete description of resources marked with an asterisk, see the Appendix.

For Alternate 1

—Bibles in various translations
—Pencils
—Writing paper
—Music sheet with words to
    "His Sheep Am I"

For Alternate 2

—Bibles in various translations
—Copies of plot for skit (to give
    out in advance to those who
    will do it)
—Copy of litany
—Glue
—Music sheet with words to
    "Amazing Grace"
—Scissors
—Newsprint
—Newspapers and magazines

Optional Resources for Both Alternatives

—*Arch Books Aloud,* "Jon and the Little Lost Lamb"
—*Lost Puppy* or *The Stray* from TeleKETICS
—*A New Now Songbook* from Hope Publishing Company, or
another songbook containing "His Sheep Am I" or "Amazing Grace"
—Record player
—16 mm film projector, extension cord, and extra bulb

Litany for Concluding Alternate 2

LEADER: We have felt like the lost sheep in many ways, alone and
    uncertain of our direction.

PEOPLE: Thank you, God, for finding us, even when we did not want
    to be found.

LEADER: We know how others who are lost may feel in their
    loneliness.

PEOPLE: Help us to seek them as you have sought us.

LEADER: We have chosen individuals and families whom we want to
    bring to you in some way this week.

PEOPLE: We need the assurance of your presence as we attempt to
    show them we care.

LEADER: Go in peace, knowing that God is with you in the tasks you
    have accepted for yourselves.

PEOPLE: We go, knowing He is with us.

ALL: Amen.

Session II.
The Parable of the King Who Forgave His Servants

THE HEAVENLY MEANING

God is more forgiving of us than we usually are of others. His forgiveness is limitless, even running the risk of Jesus' death on the cross. Thus, there should be no limit to our forgiveness of others.

THE EARTHLY STORY

In Jesus' Day

The ancient rabbis taught that a man must forgive his brother *three* times. Peter thought he was being generous when he suggested seven times. But Jesus said we should forgive seventy times seven, probably meaning to forgive without limitation.

The contrast between the two debts referred to in the parable is an exaggeration used to show why we should be willing to forgive others the little wrongs they do when we have been forgiven so often for so much. The talent referred to here was worth about a thousand dollars. So the servant owed the king about ten million dollars. The denarius was worth about twenty cents; so the servant's fellow servant owed him only twenty dollars. The exaggeration illustrates how we should be much more forgiving than we usually are.

In Our Day

For children: Most children know the endless forgiveness of their parents, even though they are often less forgiving of siblings. The learning experiences can enlarge on this background, helping them to be more forgiving of one another.

For teenagers: Teenagers are quick to detect "hypocrisy" in those who profess to know God's forgiveness, but fail to forgive others. They, like adults, are less quick to see their own inconsistencies. This parable can help them gain more awareness of their own intolerance.

For adults: Adults often rationalize their intolerance by calling for a balance between mercy and justice. In some instances this is important for an orderly society, but they should be encouraged to deal with their own problems of giving and still maintain an orderly society.

For families: The family is a good setting in which to begin applying the lesson of this parable. Family conflict often arises out of lack of tolerance among the members of the family. Most relationships can be helped greatly by a little more forgiveness.

THE LEARNING GOAL FOR THIS SESSION

Through this session the participants will gain an understanding of how much God forgives them. They will be able to relate the central lesson of the parable to one or two of their own experiences.

POSSIBLE LEARNING ACTIVITIES

Getting Started

Alternate 1

1. Ask a family to prepare a skit in advance either depicting the story of the parable in a modern setting or their own plot developed around the theme of forgiveness. The role-play situation following this session may be used or adapted.

Alternate 2

1. Play the *Arch Books Aloud* record "The Unforgiving Servant" to introduce the biblical story. (This is also available in book form and may be read aloud.)

Developing the Session

Alternate 1

1. Have each individual do a finger painting depicting feelings of being forgiven, holding a grudge, or feeling guilt. Have them use colors and designs to express emotions.

2. Give each group time to discuss their finger paintings and how guilt, forgiveness, or grudges feel. Encourage them to draw from their own experiences. If the groups are quite large, have them divide up into smaller groups, such as triads (groups of three).

Alternate 2

1. Have each small group role-play the parable or a situation in which one who has repeated an offense several times must ask for forgiveness. Keep the role play short. Encourage some humor, but do not obscure the lesson of the role play. The leader should write out clear role descriptions in advance. You may wish to think up your own or to use the situation following this session.

2. Lead a discussion on how each person felt in the roles he or she played. Let other members of the group respond.

Concluding the Session

Alternate 1

1 Invite individuals to share their paintings and feelings with the total group.

2. Sing the traditional or a contemporary version of "Amazing Grace" or "Grace Greater Than Our Sin."

3. Call for a moment of silence for group members to ask God for forgiveness of specific failures, for strength to forgive others, and to give thanks for God's forgiveness.

Alternate 2

1. Reread Matthew 18:21-22 where Jesus told Peter to forgive seventy times seven.

2. Sing "Take Our Bread," words and music by Joseph Wise (in *Songbook for Saints and Sinners*).

3. Dismiss the session with a benediction. Either make up your own or use the following: "Go, remembering what you have learned and experienced here. Take with you the awareness of God's forgiveness and love through Jesus Christ, willing and determined to pass it on to those who may wrong you. So leave and live in the name of Jesus Christ. Amen."

SUGGESTED RESOURCES FOR THIS SESSION

See the Appendix for a more complete description of resources marked with an asterisk.

For Alternate 1
—Bibles in various translations
—Copies or newsprint copy of the words to "Amazing Grace" or "Grace Greater Than Our Sin"
—Copies of role-play situations
—Finger paints in various colors
—Glazed paper, one sheet for each person, plus a few extras

For Alternate 2
—*Arch Books Aloud,* "The Unforgiving Servant" (also available in book form)
—Bibles in various translations
—Copies of role-play situations
—Record player, extension cord
—Words to "Take Our Bread" or songbooks containing the song

Optional Items
—*The Meter,* 16 mm telespot from TeleKETICS
—16 mm movie projector, extra bulb, and extension cord

Instructions for Finger Painting

Use some kind of glazed paper, such as shelf paper or butcher paper. Place the paper on several thicknesses of newspapers. Spoon the color of paint selected onto the paper; then make designs with your fingers. Hang it to dry.

Role-Play Situations

The father of the family has a habit of ignoring comments from his oldest son while discussing events of the day at the supper table. When the son grows silent, Father becomes concerned. Discovering what he has done, he asks the son to forgive him or apologizes in some way. In the process of his discussion with the older son, a younger child keeps interrupting, obviously getting on Father's nerves.

Roles:

FATHER: Disturbed because his secretary seemed to be unable to do anything right at the office, he unloads on his wife at the supper table. He ignores Jim's comments for some time, even interrupting and cutting him off. This begins the scene. When Jim becomes quiet, Father realizes that he has been ignoring him, not only tonight but also at many meals, and he seeks Jim's forgiveness. However, after Jim has accepted his father's apologies, Scott, age seven, interrupts, feeling ignored. Father then severely scolds him for being so rude.

JIM: (age sixteen) Jim is excited about the coming ball game that night and wants his dad to go to the game with him. He begins the supper discussion by sharing his excitement, which goes unheard. As his father continually dominates the discussion, Jim becomes quiet, looking rejected and withdrawn. When Father realizes his own impoliteness and seeks Jim's forgiveness, or apologizes, Jim somewhat hesitantly accepts the apology. However, when Scott interrupts and receives the scolding from Father, even after he has just apologized for doing the same thing, Jim turns on his dad for being so intolerant—expecting to be forgiven, but not willing to do so himself.

SCOTT: (age seven) Scott is quiet through most of the discussion until after Jim accepts Father's apology for ignoring him during the supper conversation. Then he tries to interrupt to tell about a project that is coming up at school, building a birdhouse. He wants to know if Father would help do it.

MOTHER: Mother is the quiet listener, trying to referee the discussion. Occasionally she tries to enter her own concerns about the next parents' project for the grade school.

This role play could be developed into a skit, or roles could be reversed with a child playing Father, another Mother, and adults playing the children's parts.

Session III.
The Parable of the Prodigal Son

THE HEAVENLY MEANING

In a sense, there are two subparables here, but both speak of the way God forgives and accepts us. If we let the older son represent a "righteous" person, the parable seems to point out that God is more merciful in his judgments than many a "righteous" person. God forgives when we refuse to forgive because he loves us far more than we love each other.

Suggested *alternate* *usage*   This parable could be used in a series with the parable of the lost sheep (Matthew 18:10-14; Luke 15:1-7) and the parable of the lost coin (Luke 15:8-10). All three deal with the love of God which causes him to seek us out. William Barclay suggests that each of these parables deals with a different reason for our being lost. The sheep got lost through *sheer foolishness.* The coin was lost *through no fault of its own.* The son became lost *by his own choice.*[3]

[3] William Barclay, *The Gospel of Luke,* The Daily Study Bible (Philadelphia: The Westminster Press, 1956), pp. 206-214.

THE EARTHLY STORY

In Jesus' Day

Under Jewish law the older son was to get two-thirds of his father's property when his father died, and the younger son one-third (Deuteronomy 21:17). It was quite common for the father to distribute his estate before he died. In this case, the younger son asked for his share in advance.

The worst employment to which a Jewish person could sink was to feed swine, for the Jewish law said, "Cursed is he who feeds swine."[4]

In Our Day

For children: Some children have had the temporary desire to run away from home. Most will know what it feels like to be forgiven and accepted by Mother or Dad after doing something wrong for which they fully expected to be punished. They should be helped to see that God's love, forgiveness, and acceptance are even greater than that of their parents.

For teenagers: This parable is probably most relevant to teenagers who are going through some of the rebelliousness of adolescence and who are trying to establish their own independence. They may find it a little more difficult to identify with the "repentance" or return of the prodigal son. The lesson for them may come in the assurance that, even when they make mistakes when "going it alone," there is still acceptance at home and with God.

For adults: Adults can remember both their childhood and teenage experiences. They will also find it helpful to reflect on how forgiving and accepting they might be if this were their son or daughter. What would their first impulse be at such a rebellion and "humble return"?

For families: There is much in this parable that can draw out feelings of the members of a family toward each other. A family discussion could result leading to some decisions about freedom, patience, dependence, independence, forgiveness, and fairness.

THE LEARNING GOAL FOR THIS SESSION

Through this session the participants will gain a deeper

[4]Quoted in *ibid.,* p. 212.

understanding of how it feels to be forgiven and accepted by God. They will learn to express this same forgiveness and acceptance more within their families. Parents will be better able to understand a teenager's need to find independence from the family.

POSSIBLE LEARNING ACTIVITIES

Getting Started

Alternate 1

1. Divide the total group into three smaller groups for a fishbowl role play. Assign each group to one of the three main characters in the parable—the father, the older son, and the younger son. Have each group appoint one of their members to play the role assigned to them. They are to role-play a discussion following the party honoring the younger son. Let the characters do the role play for awhile, then retire to separate places to consult with their "teams," then reassemble in the fishbowl formation to continue the role play.

Alternate 2

1. Appoint a family in advance to prepare a skit based on one of their own family experiences or one of the following ideas:

a. Dad or Mom receives a telephone call from the police saying their runaway son is being held.

b. The son calls home from a runaway center in a distant city.

2. If there are several younger children involved, play *Arch Books Aloud,* "The Boy Who Ran Away." (Or read the booklet by the same title.)

Developing the Session

Alternate 1

1. Discuss the role play. Let the three small groups continue separate discussions after the role play using the following questions:

   (1) How did the father feel when the son left?

   (2) How did the father feel when the son returned?

   (3) How did the younger son feel when he decided to leave? To return?

Alternate 2

1. Show the 16 mm film from TeleKETICS entitled *Workout,* the story of a difficult relationship between a father and his college-age son, with each having trouble accepting the viewpoint of the other. It deals with estrangement between parents and teenagers. It is a bit dated in dress, but still usable.

2. Have the family or group members discuss the issues they

(4) How did he feel when his father prepared the feast for him?

(5) How did the older son feel when his father had the feast for the younger son?

(6) Which son do you think was most right? Most wrong?

(7) Which character in the story do you identify with the most?

2. Let each family make a banner on which each family member puts a design expressing who he or she is or how he or she sees himself or herself in relationship with the family. They could cut out pictures or words from brightly colored felt and glue them to the burlap backing. Provide standards to use in the celebration following.

know about that cause misunderstanding between the members of their family. When discussing these issues, have parents discuss them from their children's point of view and the children from the parents' point of view. Then have each member of the group list "new learnings I have about these issues." Encourage them to think of ways they can be more understanding of the viewpoint of the other person.

Concluding the Session

Alternate 1

1. Play the song, "Free to Be You and Me" from the album by that name. This song and others on the album deal with personal identity and the freedom to be oneself.

2. Give families time to share the meaning of their banners. (They could march around the room holding their banners while "Free to Be You and Me" is playing.)

3. Sing the song by the Medical Mission Sisters, "Ballad of the Prodigal Son" from their book

Alternate 2

1. Play the song "Free to Be You and Me."

2. Give families time together to "contract" or agree with one another on ways in which they can be more tolerant, forgiving, and accepting of one another in the coming week.

3. Read from Robert Raines's book *Creative Brooding,* "I Hold the Bandages and Ointments Ready," on page 20. (The reading is followed by some relevant Scriptures and a short prayer.)

4. Sing the hymn "O Love That

entitled, *I Know the Secret.* You could sing it to the accompaniment of the record by the same name.

4. Close in prayer either using the following or one of your own: "Dear Father, forgive us for searching in the wrong places for purpose in our lives. Give us the courage to be independent, but at the same time, the assurance that we are never outside the reach of your love. In Jesus' name we pray, Amen."

Wilt Not Let Me Go" and close with a short benediction.

SUGGESTED RESOURCES FOR THIS SESSION

See the Appendix for a more complete description of resources marked with an asterisk.

For Alternate 1

—Banner materials, burlap, felt, glue, scissors, etc.
—Bibles in various translations
—Lists of discussion questions
—*Record and/or songbook, *I Know the Secret,* Medical Mission Sisters
—*Record, "Free to Be You and Me"
—Record player and extension cord

Optional Resources:

—*Purple Puzzle Tree,* set number 5 (Set includes records. Books are available separately.)

For Alternate 2

—*Arch Books Aloud,* "The Boy Who Ran Away" (or just the book)
—Bibles in various translations
—*Film, *Workout* from Tele-KETICS (*The Wanderer* may be substituted)
—Record player and extension cord
—*Robert Raines, *Creative Brooding*
—16 mm projector and extra bulb, screen, and extension cord
—Words to hymn, "O Love That Wilt Not Let Me Go"

Session IV.
The Parable of the Rich Man and Lazarus

THE HEAVENLY MEANING

This story teaches that we should be compassionate in the presence of human need, regardless of the social status of the person in need. The lack of that compassion, and not his many possessions, was the sin of the rich man. This parable is neither a blanket condemnation of the rich nor an exaltation of the poor. Rather it is a condemnation of the self-centered love, the blindness of the rich man and all like him to the realities of God's will in the presence of human need.

THE EARTHLY STORY
In Jesus' Day

Part of the ancient "welfare" system in Jesus' day was to allow those who, due to some disability, were unable to supply their own needs to sit at the doors and gates of the rich to "beg" for food. It would be unheard of to refuse to give them help. We can be sure this rich man did what society and his religious law expected of him. But he did it without compassion, and in that is his condemnation.

In Our Day

Vagrancy is against the law in many cities in our nation. Today we have government welfare programs for people like Lazarus. But too often they are hampered by so much bureaucratic red tape that the recipient is dehumanized through the process.

How often do we respond to the needs of people on welfare and do the extra thing that will help them over the hump? How often do we look down on the person who has to accept welfare or beg as someone who is to be avoided or, at best, simply tolerated? How often are the transients who come through town given the help they need? Or is it our first assumption that they are part of a large, organized racket?

Many are the comparisons that make this parable relevant to our day.

For children: Children usually have an immediate sense of fairness when they hear such a story as this or a modern parallel. They can also think of simple ways in which to help such a person. They can identify with the feelings of people caught in such circumstances as was Lazarus.

For teenagers: Teenagers are beginning to get caught in the conflict between material possessions and benevolent action for the material welfare of others. The desire for the latest styles, the newest thing in quadrophonic sound, and the latest fads compete with the feeling of personal responsibility for the needs of others. The teen years are years in which values begin to solidify in regard to material comforts and luxuries of life. And that is what this parable is about.

For adults: Adults have usually established their values regarding concern for the needs of others and acquiring of personal comforts and prosperity. They usually believe they should help others in some way, but their actions often show they actually *value* their personal prosperity most. Thus adults may have stronger feelings of guilt when they hear of others who need help, such as the thousands of people who starve each day in underdeveloped countries. Or their rationalizations for not helping are very strong and sometimes very well developed.

For families: A decision by one member of the family to sacrifice some of his or her personal comforts for the sake of someone outside the family directly affects the other members of the family. Hence this parable is an excellent one to use to help family members work together at clarifying their values and responsibilities to less fortunate persons.

THE LEARNING GOAL FOR THIS SESSION

Through this session the family members will gain a better understanding of their Christian responsibility to the poor and will decide on one or two ways in which their family can begin to show concern.

POSSIBLE LEARNING ACTIVITIES

Getting Started

Alternate 1

1. Learn the spiritual "Poor Man Lazarus."
2. Play the *Purple Puzzle Tree,* Album #5, "The Rich Man and Lazarus," to introduce the parable.

Alternate 2

1. Show the film *The Puzzle,* from TeleKETICS. A high-powered executive collides with a small "nobody" boy in a busy airport. His decision to come back and help gather the child's scattered puzzle pieces evokes the memorable question, "Are you God?" (60 sec.)

Developing the Session

Alternate 1

1. Invite a social worker to spend some time with the group to tell about his or her work with people, or visit a Christian center and conduct this entire program there.
2. If time permits, have the family groups make collages showing the contrast between poverty and wealth, using pictures and headlines out of magazines and newspapers.
3. Allow time for participants to brainstorm things they might do, especially as a family, to be more

Alternate 2

1. Do one of the simulation games, "Poverty" or "Star Power." Both show the dynamics of poverty amid affluence. "Poverty" is a bit simpler than "Star Power." Both are too complex for younger children, so alternate play activities should be planned for them if these games are used. (See Appendix for descriptions of the games and where to get them.)
2. If these simulation games are not available to you, have a small group or groups role-play or

responsive to the needs of the poor in their community. Encourage them to think of something that has a more lasting effect than the "Christmas basket" kind of ideas. Ask them to make a symbol of their project for the closing of the session.

pantomime the parable or a modern version of it. You could have each family unit develop its own skit.

3. Have the small groups reflect on and discuss their feelings regarding poverty and plenty.

4. Allow time for participants to decide on projects for the next week. Offer some specific suggestions and information, such as your denominational hunger resources. Other possible ideas could be information on WHEAT, Project Heifer, Church World Service, Share Bread, etc.

As a third alternative, continue the session for two meetings, using parts of both Alternates 1 and 2 for beginning the sessions. For developing the second session, have reports from families on things that were done. Follow the reports by concluding the second session with a celebration of "what God has done through us to help others." Include some of the concluding activities listed below.

Concluding the Session

Alternate 1

1. As a devotional thought, read from Luke 18:18-30 about the rich young ruler who came to Jesus.

2. Have each group share what group members plan to do the coming week to show that they care about the poor. Have them place their symbol of that idea on a large collage or mural.

3. Sing the hymn "Take My Life and Let It Be" or sing "Poor Man Lazarus" again.

Alternate 2

1. Play the *Purple Puzzle Tree* set number 5, "When Jesus Told His Parables of Love."

2. Ask participants to share what they hope to do for a project.

3. Sing "Take Our Bread" from the *Songbook for Saints and Sinners*.

4. Close with a prayer of commitment, such as: "Our Father, you have taught us that we cannot live by bread alone,

4. Close with a prayer of commitment, such as the following: "Our Father in heaven, you have heard our intentions and seen the symbols we have made. Help us, we pray, to bring them to life this week as we attempt to care for the needy. Amen." but we are also aware that many need physical bread just to keep alive. Help us to be the source of that bread for others so they may also find food for the spirit. Amen."

SUGGESTED RESOURCES FOR THIS SESSION

See the Appendix for a more complete description of resources marked with an asterisk.

For Alternate 1

—*Album #5, *The Purple Puzzle Tree,* "The Rich Man and Lazarus"
—Construction paper or material scraps for symbols
—Glue
—Large newsprint for mural
—Old magazines and newspapers
—Record player and extension cord
—Scissors
—*Songbooks or song sheets with words to "Take My Life and Let It Be"
—Song sheet for the spiritual "Poor Man Lazarus," available from Bourne Music Publishers, 1212 Avenue of the Americas, New York, NY 10036

For Alternate 2

—Bibles in various paraphrases
—Old clothes for skit costumes
—**Purple Puzzle Tree,* Set number 5
—**The Puzzle,* from TeleKET-ICS
—Record player and extension cord
—*Simulation game, either "Star Power" or "Poverty"
—*Songbooks or song sheets with words to "Take Our Bread" from *Songbook for Saints and Sinners*

Session V.
The Parable of the Pharisee and the Tax Collector

THE HEAVENLY MEANING

This parable is directed toward those who think they are more righteous than someone else. It teaches the importance of humility before persons and God, especially in our acts of worship.

The prayer of the tax collector, "O God, be merciful to me—a sinner!" receives much more attention from God than the self-righteous prayer of the Pharisee in which he tells God how good he is.

There is an appropriate place for a healthy kind of pride and self-respect for the Christian, but not at the expense of degrading others.

THE EARTHLY STORY
In Jesus' Day

Only one fast was required by the Jewish law. That was on the Day of Atonement. Those, like this Pharisee, who wished to gain special merit fasted also on Mondays and Thursdays because these were market days when people from all over the country were in Jerusalem, thus giving the self-righteous man a large audience.

This Pharisee also tithed things he was not obligated to tithe.

The Levites were to receive only a tithe of all a man's agricultural produce (Numbers 18:21; Deuteronomy 14:22).

In Our Day

For children: Some children are spoiled and have a vain image of themselves. But other children are so humiliated by their parents in front of other people (what parent wants to be embarrassed by a show-off?) that they have not learned the healthy ways in which to love themselves. They tend to do it by competition with others and by putting them down. This parable also speaks strongly about prayer and worship. It can be used to help children know what attitude they should have when they pray or worship.

For teenagers: What teenager has not been bored by the typical worship services, the long prayers and the complicated sermons? This parable speaks about authentic worship. On the other hand, many youth seem to be searching for something that has "spiritual" significance. Many young people who still choose to remain in the organized church seem to be looking for some kind of mystical experience. Others are completely turned off by such "weird" things. One thing common to teens is the search for self-identity, part of which is the process of comparing oneself to others to see how the self measures up. That is not all bad. In fact, it is necessary to have models with which to compare oneself. This parable can be used to help teens find healthy standards for self-measurement, plus an authentic means of prayer and worship.

For adults: Many adults have tried various ways of praying, but few break through the barriers of artificial phraseology and become free to be honest with themselves and with God in prayer. The specific application of this parable would be to attain honesty and accuracy in one's view of himself or herself as compared to others. But the application can be made broader to include honesty about one's feelings toward stressful situations.

For families: Many families either ignore family worship altogether or struggle to find honest forms of family worship which are enriching to them. They should be encouraged to evaluate their family relationships to see if they reflect the results of their worship.

THE LEARNING GOAL FOR THIS SESSION

Through this session the participants will have a greater understanding of true humility and how it is reflected in worship of God and relationships with others. They will begin to apply what they learn in their own worship. (This is based on the assumption that true humility consists of a position between thinking too highly of oneself on the one hand and thinking too lowly of oneself on the other.)

POSSIBLE LEARNING ACTIVITIES
Getting Started

Alternate 1

1. Have two people prepare a skit in advance to introduce the content of the parable, using plenty of imagination and humor. (See resources at the end of this session for a suggested skit.)
2. Read or tell the story, from *George and Other Parables* by Patricia Ryan (Argus Communications), about George, whose exaggerated sense of importance proves to be his undoing.

Alternate 2

1. Play "Two Men in the Temple" from *Arch Books Aloud* (or read the story).
2. Read or tell the story *I Am Loveable and Capable,* from Argus Communications. Have participants make and decorate their own IALAC signs as described in the story.

Developing the Session

Alternate 1

1. Ask participants to select partners who are not members of their families or who have not been grouped with them in prior sessions. While the entire group is still together, but after participants have selected partners, have them listen to "Free to Be You and Me" (even if you have used it in Session III).
2. Instruct participants to take five or ten minutes to discuss the following with their partners:
a. Share one thing they don't like about themselves.
b. Share one thing they like very

Alternate 2

1. Divide the people into two or three age groups—adults, teens, children. Then do the following:
a. Have the adults and teens who are at least juniors in high school write a resumé applying for a position with some important firm, indicating why they think they are qualified for the job.
b. Have the younger ones express in some way why they should be included on a team in a game of softball for neighborhood kids. For the smaller children it may be best for one

much about themselves.

3. Have the groups of two form groups of four and discuss how they felt about sharing good things about themselves, then how they felt about sharing things they did not like about themselves.

4. Have participants fill out the self-assessment form at the end of this session. (Parents could work with their younger children.)

adult to lead them in a discussion on how they would try to convince their mother that they deserve an extra cookie.

2. Have the participants, either individually or in teams, translate or change their ideas into prayers to God which are in keeping with the prayer of the tax collector.

This may be a good session to let the adults be favored on their level since often the tendency is to adjust everything to the youngest. If you decide to do this, before moving on to the conclusion of the session, have them discuss what it means to be humble in prayer. Be sure to have alternate activities for children since the discussion will go over their heads. A play corner with quiet toys in one corner of the room where the group is meeting would be best. Coloring sheets would also be helpful. These could be duplicated, or coloring books could be used.

Concluding the Session

Alternate 1

1. Read Psalm 8 from a modern translation or paraphrase, such as *God Is Here, Let's Celebrate,* by Leslie F. Brandt.

2. Allow time for silent prayers and meditation, suggesting a few things to think about, such as "How honest are you in your worship?" "Can you express your anger to God?" "Do you feel free to pray to God or is he unreachable?" "Are you free from judging others in your prayers?" (Delay a few seconds

Alternate 2

1. Read the parable again from a modern translation, such as the *New English Bible.*

2. Invite participants to share their prayers which they wrote during this session; however, do not push them.

3. Close by singing "Sweet Hour of Prayer" or "Take Time to Be Holy," found in most hymnals.

between each question.)

3. Offer a prayer asking God to hear the thoughts "we have just meditated upon as our prayers."

4. Close by singing "Hear Our Prayer, O Lord" or "Spirit of the Living God, Fall Afresh on Me."

SUGGESTED RESOURCES FOR THIS SESSION

See the Appendix for a more complete description of resources marked with an asterisk.

For Alternate 1

—Bibles in various translations
—*George and Other Parables* by Patricia Ryan
—Newsprint with discussion questions listed (optional)
—*Paraphrase of Psalm 8, *God Is Here, Let's Celebrate,* by Leslie F. Brandt
—*Record "Free to Be You and Me"
—Record player, extension cord
—Self-assessment forms
—Song sheets with words to "Hear Our Prayer, O Lord" or "Spirit of the Living God" (Both songs are found in *Youth Sings,* Gospel Light Publications, P.O. Box 1680, Glendale, CA 91209.)
—Two copies of the skit below

For Alternate 2

—*Arch Books Aloud* "Two Men in the Temple," or just the book
—Bibles in various translations
—*Copy of "I Am Loveable and Capable" from Argus Communications
—Paper, crayons, and pencils for writing and making IALAC signs
—Record player, extension cord
—*Song sheets with words to "Sweet Hour of Prayer" or "Take Time to Be Holy," found in most hymnals

Skit for Alternate 1

The scene is a place of worship. The first person should be dressed in rags and the other in fine clothes.

FIRST PERSON: God, I really feel lousy. I'm almost afraid to talk to you; I've been so rotten. I lost my temper and slugged a friend today. . . .

SECOND PERSON: Almighty God, our Father, I beseech Thee to look upon my countenance with pleasure and my disposition with approval, for in this day Thou gavest me the strength to be kind in the face of my adversary, and thus enabled me to gain the upper hand.

FIRST PERSON: I don't really even know how to talk to you. This guy standing next to me seems to say everything so nice; so I'm sure he makes quite an impression on you. But I get all tongue-tied trying to use his lingo. I sure hope you can understand what I'm trying to say.

SECOND PERSON: I thank Thee, O Lord Most High, exalted above all men, that Thou hast blessed me with the eloquence of tongue so that I may address Thee with dignity and distinction, and not in the gutteral doggerel of this lowly outcast who attempts to gain your recognition.

FIRST PERSON: I'm not even sure what to call you, but if you are really God, I hope you are listening. I know I shouldn't expect it. I ain't been to church for a he . . . pardon me . . . a very long time. Of course, the truth is, I'm kind of embarrassed to come with these rags I have on. They sure ain't "Sunday-go-to-meetin'." duds. But it's all I got. I know this religious fellow over here has pleased you, seein' as how he's got a string of perfect attendance pins hanging down to his knees. Sorry I ain't like him, but I hope you will at least try to understand.

SECOND PERSON: Thou hast blessed me with the ability and determination to serve Thee. Unlike this irregular beggar, I have been perfect in my attendance at worship. And I thank Thee that I have the respect for Thy house not to disgrace it by wearing unclean rags.

FIRST PERSON: I know you don't owe me anything. I only have a quarter to put in the collection. I guess I kind of wasted my money on some booze last night. Sorry about that, God, but I just couldn't help myself.

SECOND PERSON: Thou hast blessed me with the spirit of benevolent charity. Unlike this wretched sinner here, I tithe all that I have, even before taxes. I say my prayers regularly and in public places so that others may learn how to pray by following my fine example.

FIRST PERSON: Thanks, God, for not hitting me with lightning or striking me dead for having the gall to come to you like this, but I needed to talk to you and was hoping that you would let me know somehow that you love me, even though I feel so rotten inside.

THE VOICE OF GOD: It's all right, friend. I know you hurt, but I hear you. Always remember, you're my child, and I love you no matter how rotten you are.

SECOND PERSON: And finally, I beseech Thee, most wise and knowledgeable God, accept my praise and supplication in the spirit in which it is given.

THE VOICE OF GOD : You, there, in those fancy duds. I'm not deaf, but for some reason, the message is garbled. Did you say something, or are you just warming up to the subject?

Self-Assessment Instrument for Alternate 1

1. Score yourself in Column 1 from 1 to 10 on how you rate on each of the following questions, 1 being low and 10 high.
2. After you finish scoring yourself in Column 1, go back through the questions and place a score in Column 2 indicating how you would like to rate. Be realistic.
3. Subtract the highest score from the lowest, regardless of which column they appear in. Place the difference in Column 3. This is your "growth score." (Example: On question 1, assume the score in Column 1 is 4 and the score in Column 2 is 6. The "growth score" in Column 3 would be 2, the difference between 4 and 6.)
4. Total each column for total scores.

	Column 1	Column 2	Column 3
1. I am able to observe other people's actions without judging them.	_____	_____	_____
2. I can discuss things I like about myself without feeling egotistical.	_____	_____	_____
3. I can have my weak points called to my attention without feeling defensive.	_____	_____	_____
4. I can assert my opinion in a discus-			

sion without putting the other
person down.   _____ _____ _____

5. I can listen to the other person's
concerns or ideas without needing
to argue the point he or she is
making.   _____ _____ _____

6. If I feel my rights are being denied, I
can stand up for myself.   _____ _____ _____

7. I am honest in my worship. (I
express both positive and negative
feelings freely.)   _____ _____ _____

8. I can express my anger to God.   _____ _____ _____

9. I feel God hears me when I pray.   _____ _____ _____

10. I am free from judging others in my
prayers.   _____ _____ _____

TOTAL SCORES _____ _____ _____

Session VI.
The Parable of the Talents

THE HEAVENLY MEANING

In some ways this is a difficult parable to interpret because it seems to imply that the rich will get richer and the poor, poorer. But that is not really the point. Probably the most logical meaning is that the person who is entrusted with gifts, whether they be wealth, abilities, or knowledge, and who takes risks to exercise those gifts, will find them increased. The person who hoards his or her gifts will find they dwindle away.

THE EARTHLY STORY
In Jesus' Day

The situation that inspired Jesus to relate this parable was probably that of the scribes and Pharisees whose aim it was to keep the law exactly as it was. Like the man with one talent, they tried to keep things exactly as they were by resisting any change, any development, any alteration, or any innovation. For that they are condemned. Any religion without adventurous faith or with a shut mind has no possibility of being relevant to the age in which it exists.

In Our Day

The most obvious application of this parable would be to correct the tendency to protect the status quo in religious belief and practice simply because that is the way it has always been done. But it can also be applied specifically to the use of gifts.

For children: Children are often possessive of their own toys and belongings and need to be helped to see that through sharing what they have, even at the risk of losing it or having it damaged, the pleasure increases. Belongings become important not in and of themselves, but because of the relationships they can be used to help build.

For teenagers: Teenagers are beginning to discover their gifts and becoming more aware of their abilities. But they often are not quite sure how to use them responsibly or productively. They need encouragement to discover their abilities and to use them.

For adults: Many adults are very reluctant to take risks to try something new, especially if it might threaten their security. Faith consists of the willingness to take risks in life, and they need encouragement to do so.

For families: The family can offer the security needed to encourage each member to try something new. The family can be there as a place to return where there is warmth and acceptance, especially if the risk results in failure. The family members can also encourage one another to try again.

THE LEARNING GOAL FOR THIS SESSION

As a result of this session the participants will be more willing to take a risk in at least one area of their ability where normally they would not. Through the session they will become more aware of their own potential.

POSSIBLE LEARNING ACTIVITIES

If you have avoided the expense of using some of the 16 mm films recommended in previous sessions, it may be wise to "take a risk" at this point and use some extra resources for this session for two reasons. First, the sessions have been arranged in such an order that they build toward helping a person move toward his or her own potential; so this session is a climax. Second, this is the last session, and there should be some kind of extra celebration to "seal off" the total experience.

It would be a good idea to plan for extra time for this session, especially the conclusion. You are not only concluding one session but also the entire six-session unit. This calls for a special celebration at the end. If this session is held during good weather, combine it with a picnic in an area where you have a lodge that can be darkened for films, unless you do not plan to use any.

Getting Started

Alternate 1

1. As participants enter the room, ask them to draw a picture on a piece of construction paper indicating an ability they have. The paper should be large enough for small children to draw something, but small enough so it can be pinned to their clothing or hung around their neck with a piece of yarn. Provide crayons, felt-tip markers, and tempera paint in egg cartons for this activity.
2. Introduce the parable by playing the *Arch Books Aloud* record, "Eight Bags of Gold," or read the book aloud.

Alternate 2

1. Have someone tell the story *Hope for the Flowers,* by Trina Paulus, or the story from *George and Other Parables,* by Patricia Ryan, about Mary Alice, who decides to bank her carefully guarded potential. (*Hope for the Flowers* is rather long; so it should be condensed or extra time should be allowed.)
2. Read the parable from a modern translation or a paraphrase. Or read it from *Arch Books,* "Eight Bags of Gold."

Developing the Session

Alternate 1

1. Divide into smaller groups and have each one share with the rest of the group the meaning of the picture he or she drew in the beginning of the session.
2. Distribute *unequal* amounts of art materials to each person in each of the small groups and instruct them to "create" some-

Alternate 2

1. Divide into smaller groups of not more than three to five in each group. Ask them to take a walk in the picnic area and look for objects they can use to create a three-dimensional picture of themselves. For example, if they feel a bit uncertain about their future, they may select a piece of

thing using only the material they were given and their own imaginations. It does not need to have any special religious significance. It is to be their own creation.

3. Give them time to share their "creations" with one another in their group by showing them and explaining them.

4. Have a brief discussion on how it feels to create something using only what has been given you.

sandstone as a base. Allow adequate time and provide glue or other needed tools for them to create their picture.

2. Give them time to share their "creations" with others in their group by showing them and explaining them.

Concluding the Session

Remember that this is a conclusion for the whole unit.

Alternate 1

1. Show the 16 mm film, *William,* from TeleKETICS. William is a six-year-old boy who is too big to be a baby and too small to be "one of the guys," but who finds his own way to become the "hero" at the picnic when he finds a lost diamond without even looking for it. If this film is not available, you may wish to use *A Talent for Tony* or the filmstrip *The Magic Sampo,* both from TeleKETICS.

2. Have the participants put up all of the projects, banners, murals, pictures, etc., that they have made in prior sessions as a celebration of what has happened during their time together.

3. Sing "Take Our Bread" from *Songbook for Saints and Sinners.*

Alternate 2

1. If you are near a sheltered place where projects can be taped to the wall or hung, do the same as in step 2 of Alternate 1. Otherwise, take time for reflection on what has happened during the past sessions. Do it in several rounds by asking each person first to recall something funny that happened to him or her in one of the sessions. Have each name his or her favorite parable of the six studied and give reasons why. Have each name one important thing he or she learned and why it is important.

2. Sing the hymn "Take My Life and Let It Be" or "Just As I Am."

3. For a closing prayer give God thanks for all the experiences that have been mentioned. Ask

4. For a closing prayer ask people to mention spontaneously in one short sentence something they have experienced during the sessions for which they are thankful. After each statement have the entire group respond with the phrase "We give you thanks, O God." Then close with the following benediction or charge: "Return, now, to your families, jobs, and daily opportunities knowing that God will enable you to do them better because of what we have all learned and experienced together. Amen."

for continued motivation to live by what has been learned. Close with the following benediction or charge: "Go, now, to your own lives and destinies, knowing that God is with you and will help you to live by the new understanding you have of his Word. Amen."

You may like to keep several of the objects that have been made to display at the church for a few weeks as an encouragement to others to enlist in your next cluster event. Then return them to those who made them.

SUGGESTED RESOURCES FOR THIS SESSION

See the Appendix for a more complete description of resources marked with an asterisk.

For Alternate 1:
—*Arch Books Aloud* record, "Eight Bags of Gold"
—Bibles in various translations
—Construction paper
—Crayons
—Egg cartons
—Extension cord
—Felt-tip markers
—Filmstrip projector, extra bulb
—Miscellaneous art and craft materials, junk, etc.
—Projects from past sessions

For Alternate 2:
—*Arch Books,* "Eight Bags of Gold"
—Bibles in various translations
—*Book, *Hope for the Flowers* or *George and Other Parables*
—Glue
—Hammers and nails
—Projects from past sessions if you have a place to hang them
—Song sheets with words to "Take My Life and Let It Be," or "Just As I Am"

—Record player
—*William* from TeleKETICS
(or substitute *A Talent for
Tony* or *The Magic Sampo*)
—16 mm projector, extra bulb
—*Songbook for Saints and
Sinners* or song sheets with
words of "Take Our Bread"

Appendix I.
Family Cluster Retreat

Purpose: To provide participating families and individuals opportunities for:
1. *Experiencing* a family cluster learning event.
2. *Training* in leading a family cluster learning event:
    a. Planning the session.
    b. Leading the session.
    c. Evaluating the session.

PROGRAM AND SCHEDULE (schedule should remain flexible):
Friday

6:30 P.M. Potluck supper at the church (each family is to bring a main dish, salad, and dessert).

7:30 P.M. to 8:30 P.M. Get-acquainted activities.

Squirm Tournament: Have families group together. Give each person a rubber band. Instruct them to place the rubber band over their heads, below the hair line in the back, and on the tip of the nose in the front. The object is to move the rubber band from the nose down over the mouth and chin and around the neck by means of the face muscles *only*.

Have the families do it together; then have the winners in each family compete with one another for the final winner. Encourage cheering. This is a good warmer-upper.

My Family and I: Have each family meet together. Provide a large piece of construction paper, crayons, tempera paints, yarn, etc., for each person. Punch holes in two corners of the paper. Ask each participant to draw a picture or make some symbol of several things he or she likes to do with the rest of the family.

Group families together by twos (two families) and have each member of each family share what he or she likes to do, or simply have everyone mingle with the entire group and share their symbols.

Add other get-acquainted games of your choice.

8:30 P.M. Bedtime and optional activities. Send the younger children to bed. Provide plenty of table games or have families bring games. Provide for a television, snacks, and a place where people can visit for the rest of the evening.

Saturday

8:00 A.M. Breakfast (Participants take turns preparing meals. Cover the cost of food with a registration fee.)

9:30 A.M. *Family Cluster Learning Experience I* (led by an experienced leader):

"It's Neat to Be You and Me"

11:00 A.M. Recreation and meal preparation.

Give each family materials for making kites. Have them make one or more kites, decorate them as they please, and fly them together or in competition with other families.

12:00 P.M. Lunch Time.

Put up a large sheet of newsprint with the words written at the top: "I wish after supper we could . . ." Instruct participants to write in things they would like to do after supper.

1:00 P.M. Rest, relaxation, recreation.

2:00 P.M. Evaluation and further orientation with adults and teenagers.

2:20 P.M. *Family Cluster Learning Experience II* (led by the retreat leader and one of the families): "Noah's Trauma"

4:00 P.M. Free time, recreation, meal preparation, evaluation, planning for Experience III.

5:00 P.M. Supper (barbecue).

6:00 P.M. Planning of next Family Cluster Experience, more orientation, contracting on future events of the group.

7:00 P.M. Fellowship activities (based on input at noon on the newsprint sheet "I wish after supper we could . . .").

8:30 P.M. Bedtime for young, optional activities, games, etc.

Sunday

7:00 A.M. Breakfast.

8:30 A.M. Move to another location for the rest of the session to avoid interfering with regular church activities.

9:30 A.M. *Family Cluster Learning Experience III* (led by family participants): "The Parable of the Good Samaritan" (Luke 10:25-37)

11:00 A.M. Closing Celebration (led either by the retreat leader or the pastor if he is a participant). The celebration should capture the high points of the entire retreat in a sense of gratitude for what has happened and call for a commitment to what is planned ahead for the cluster.

11:30 A.M. Adjourn.

Family Cluster Experience I
"It's Neat to Be You and Me"
(John 1:1-5)

Our God is One who created all things. He is not subject to nature but controls it. He has created us in his image and given us the opportunity and the responsibility to continue his creation. He has given us specific gifts, unique to each of us, to carry out this responsibility.

LEARNING GOAL FOR THIS SESSION

As a result of this session participants should be able to show their understanding of their place in God's world by illustrating one or two things they find fulfillment in doing.

POSSIBLE LEARNING ACTIVITIES
Getting Started
1. Play "Creation" from "God's Trombones."
2. Show the film *William* from TeleKETICS.

Developing the Session
1. Tell the story *I Am Loveable and Capable* by Sidney Simon.
2. Have participants gather into family groups and make a mural of how they would create the world.
3. Ask them to share their murals with other family groups.

Concluding the Session
1. Show the film *William* again.
2. Ask people to share what they have learned about themselves.
3. Sing "He's Got the Whole World in His Hands."
4. Close with a prayer of thanks for the special gifts God has given each person.

SUGGESTED RESOURCES FOR THIS SESSION
—Art supplies
—Bibles in various translations
—Butcher paper for murals
—*I Am Loveable and Capable* by Sidney Simon, Argus Communications, 7440 Natchez Avenue, Niles, IL 60648
—Record of "Creation" from "God's Trombones"
—Record player and extension cord
—16mm projector, extension cord, extra bulb, and screen
—Song, "He's Got the Whole World in His Hands"

Family Cluster Experience II
"Noah's Trauma"
LEARNING GOAL FOR THIS SESSION
As a result of this experience participants will be able to describe

how Noah and his family felt when: (1) God said, "You're it"; (2) Noah was building the ark; (3) it started to rain; (4) they were all alone during the storm; and (5) they landed on dry ground. Participants will be able to relate these feelings to their own situations.

POSSIBLE LEARNING ACTIVITIES

Getting Started

1. Sing the fun song "Noah, He Built Him an Arky."
2. Play the record by Bill Cosby, "Noah."

Developing the Session

1. Divide by families and give each family the assignment of creating a skit showing how Noah's family felt in one of the following times (each family is to take a different event):
    a. When God said, "You're it!"
    b. When Noah was building the ark.
    c. When it started to rain.
    d. When they were all alone during the storm.
    e. When they landed on dry ground.
2. Have each family present its skit.
3. Discuss feelings each one had.
4. Have each family group make a mural to show its own similar feelings. If this seems too difficult for the younger children, either have the parents help them identify feelings and find ways to symbolize them, or provide an alternate activity. A good alternate would be to have the children cut pictures of animals from magazines and glue them to large cardboard boxes.

Concluding the Session

1. Share murals with each other, interpreting them to the entire group.
2. Give thanks for feelings by asking people simply to say spontaneously, "Thank you, God, for the feeling of _____." (Suggest a few feelings like fear, hope, relief, love, forgiveness, anger, or patience.)
3. Sing, "Thank You" (in *Folk Hymnal for the Now Generation,* or other youth songbooks).

SUGGESTED RESOURCES FOR THIS SESSION

—Art supplies
—Bibles in various translations
—Large cardboard boxes
—Music sheets for "Noah, He Made Him an Arky" and "Thank You"
—Newsprint
—Magazines with pictures of animals
—Record of "Noah" by Bill Cosby
—Record player and extension cord

Family Cluster Experience III
"The Parable of the Good Samaritan"
(Luke 10:25-37)

THE HEAVENLY MEANING

At their worst, some of the Jewish rabbis narrowly confined the word *neighbor* to their *fellow Jews*. Sometimes they regarded it a sin to give help to a Gentile woman during childbirth because that would be helping to bring another Gentile into the world.

This parable tells us that love must know no limits of race. The person who needs me is my neighbor. The person whom at the given time and place I can help with my active love is my neighbor and I am his or her neighbor.

THE EARTHLY STORY

In Jesus' Day

The road from Jericho to Jerusalem was a road of narrow, rocky defiles and of hairpin turns which made it an easy place for robbers to ambush travelers. It dropped 3,600 feet in less than 20 miles.

The Samaritan history is too complex to include here and unnecessary in understanding the parable. They were basically of mixed heritage with a heathen core. They followed ancient customs of worship that were rejected by the Israelites, but some Israelites (Jews) intermarried with them, thus, their mixed heritage. The religious Jews regarded intermarriage with Gentiles such as the Samaritans with contempt.

Jesus chooses a person whom the Jews hate most, pictures him helping a Jew, and thus illustrates that love for our neighbors knows no limits.

IN OUR DAY

For children: Children are quite honest about whom they like and whom they dislike. They need a great deal of encouragement to act in a loving way toward those they don't like.

For teenagers: Peer relationships are very important among most teenagers. It is important to be with the "in group." To show kindness to someone outside the peer group invites ridicule. Teenagers often reflect very strongly the prejudices learned in early childhood from adults they have observed. They need to be encouraged to take the risk of being ridiculed by their peers in order to show compassion to those who are "despised" by their own group.

For adults: Adults vary a lot in their tendency to help only friends and their willingness to help others whom they find "undesirable." However, too often our help is impersonal. We don't want to get involved. That requires too much from us. Adults need to see the value of being willing to take such risks.

For families: Sometimes family members need help being "neighborly" to each other. Most important, however, the family can be the supportive unit that gives its members strength and courage to take the risks necessary to get involved with people outside the family group in caring relationships.

LEARNING GOAL FOR THIS SESSION

Through this session the participants will be able to show an understanding of the meaning of the parable by comparing it to one or two of their own experiences.

POSSIBLE LEARNING ACTIVITIES

Getting Started

1. Read the parable from a modern translation and have groups discuss their own understanding of the meaning.
2. Appoint a person in advance to paraphrase the parable so that it reflects the culture of the participants. For example, the good Samaritan could be a member of a minority group

that everyone can identify. The setting could be their own community, and the plot could be developed from recent local newspaper headlines.
3. Leader, give some background information from notes on **THE HEAVENLY MEANING** and **THE EARTHLY MEANING.**

Developing the Session
1. Have cluster groups discuss the meaning of the parable for today.
2. Let cluster groups choose a medium for illustrating the meaning of the story in a modern setting (collage, skit, mural, puppet show).

Concluding the Session
1. Have cluster groups share their project with other groups.
2. Have someone tell the story of "The Warm Fuzzies." (A "fuzzy" could be used as a symbol of a "good neighborly deed.")
3. Conclude with a song, a time to give "warm fuzzies," and a fellowship prayer.

RESOURCES NEEDED FOR THIS SESSION
—Art materials (tempera paints, brushes, newsprint, crayons, colored paper, glue, etc.)
—Bibles in various translations
—Large cardboard appliance box for puppet stage
—Old clothes for costumes
—Old socks for puppets
—Old magazines with pictures
—Record player, extension cord
—Story of "Warm Fuzzies" adapted from *Fuzzies, a Folk Fable for All Ages,* by Richard Lessor (Niles, Ill.: Argus Communications, 1971)
—Song sheet or songbooks for closing song

Appendix II.
Resources

Books on Methods

Calhoun, Mary, *Vacation Time, Leisure Time, Any Time You Choose.* Nashville: Abingdon Press, 1975.

A planning guide for planning family recreational activities, especially during the summer. May be helpful in planning a family cluster retreat.

Mager, Robert F., *Preparing Instructional Objectives.* Belmont, Calif.: Fearon Publishers, Inc., 1962.

An excellent guide in preparing learning goals for each session.

Rozeboom, John D., *Family Camping—Five Designs for Your Church.* Nashville: Board of Discipleship of the United Methodist Church, 1973.

A short book giving suggestions for family camping and summer retreats. Helpful for designing a summer family retreat.

Wankelman, Willard F.; Wigg, Philip; and Wigg, Marietta; *A Handbook of Arts and Crafts for Elementary and Junior High*

School Teachers. Dubuque, Iowa: William C. Brown Company, Publishers, 1968.

A very complete resource book on many, many forms of art and craft media, including bulletin boards, ceramics, chalk, crayon, lettering, murals, paint and ink, paper and cardboard, printing processes, sculpture, stencils, textiles. 253 pages.

Books for Singing

Favorite Hymns of Praise. Chicago: Hope Publishing Company, 1967.

A church worship hymnal which contains many of the old favorite hymns, including all those mentioned in these sessions.

A New Now Songbook. Chicago: Hope Publishing Company, 1971.

A collection of old and new hymns and choruses.

Youth Sings. Glendale, Calif.: Gospel Light Publishers, 1951.

Contains many of the older favorite choruses.

Brown, Charles F., *Sing 'n Celebrate!* Waco, Tex.: Word, Inc., 1971.

A collection of songs by Kurt Kaiser, Sonny Salsbury, and Billy Ray Hearn.

Johnson, Norman, and Peterson, John W., *Folk Hymnal.* Grand Rapids, Mich.: Singspiration Inc., a division of The Zondervan Corporation, 1970.

A collection of old and new hymns and choruses.

Winter, Sister Miriam Therese, *I Know the Secret.* New York: Vanguard Music Corporation.

Contains the original songs as sung by the Medical Mission Sisters, including "He Bought the Whole Field," "I Know the Secret," "Don't Worry," "Ballad of the Prodigal Son," "God Loves a Cheerful Giver," "Come, Lord Jesus," "Peter," "A Virgin," "Easter Song," "Christ Is My Rock," "Come to the Springs of Living Water."

Young, Carlton R., *The Genesis Songbook.* Carol Stream, Ill.: Agape, a division of Hope Publishing Company, 1973.

Includes old and new, sacred and secular, songs.

Young, Carlton R., *Songbook for Saints and Sinners.* Carol Stream, Ill.: Agape, a division of Hope Publishing Company, 1971.

More of the same type of songs as contained in *The Genesis Songbook.*

Simulation Games

Egbert, Jim, *The Poverty Game,* available from the author of the game, at the Pilgrim United Church of Christ, 4418 Bridgetown Road, Cincinnati, OH 45211.

The game shows the dynamics of poverty in affluence. Although this is only a "game," the dynamics of the group involved in playing it are very comparable to that of the real life situation. Feelings and attitudes must be dealt with in order for the game to have any meaning.

Shirts, Garry R., *Star Power,* 1969, Simile II, 218 12th, Del Mar, CA 92014 ($3.00).

This is a game in which a low mobility three-tiered society is built through the distribution of wealth in the form of chips. Participants have a chance of progress from one level of society to another by acquiring wealth through trading with other participants. Once the society is established, the group with most wealth is given the right to make the rules for the game. The game is useful for raising questions about the use of power in a competitive society.

Storybooks

Arch Books, St. Louis, Mo.: Concordia Publishing House (See the description of *Arch Books Aloud!* under *Records* in this Appendix.)

Brandt, Leslie F., *God Is Here—Let's Celebrate.* St. Louis, Mo.: Concordia Publishing House, 1969.

Includes paraphrases of several psalms which would be usable in worship services or closing sessions.

Raines, Robert, ed. *Creative Brooding.* New York: Macmillan, Inc., 1966.

Contains several readings from contemporary literature with

related Scripture and prayers. Good for short worship or celebration events.

Ryan, Patricia, *George and Other Parables.* Niles, Ill.: Argus Communications, 1972.

Eight clever, humorous portraits of common, human idiosyncrasies, written and illustrated by Patricia Ryan. It explores what it is to be human and involved with others. Among the characters are George, whose exaggerated sense of importance proves to be his undoing, and Mary Alice, who decides to bank her carefully guarded potential.

Paulus, Trina, *Hope for the Flowers.* New York: Paulist Press, 1972.

A modern fable about two caterpillars who, after trying for wrong goals, discover their true potential as butterflies and thus bring hope to the flowers by carrying pollen from one flower to another.

Simon, Sidney B., *I Am Loveable and Capable.* Niles, Ill.: Argus Communications, 1974.

A modern allegory on the classical put-down. It is a thirty-one-page booklet containing the IALAC story and some directions of ways to use it.

Films

Lost Puppy, A Churchill Film from TeleKETICS, Franciscan Communications Center, 1229 South Santee St., Los Angeles, CA 90015.

When her puppy, Peso, runs away, Lauren becomes involved in an entangling series of episodes requiring her to think for herself and at the same time face the consequences of her decisions. Leaving her yard to look for the puppy in a nearby park, she confronts a stranger who offers her a ride in his car. She refuses and continues to search, ultimately finding Peso in a bus yard where children are not allowed. Disregarding the "keep out" sign, she retrieves her puppy and returns home, where her mother's voice brings her to a deeper realization of her actions. Recommended for primary age children. 14 minutes.

The Meter: Telespot from TeleKETICS.

An expired parking meter, a dutiful meter maid, and a nickel from a passing stranger create a charming story that symbolizes everyone's need to receive a second chance. 30 seconds.

Not for a Million: Telespot from TeleKETICS.

A leper's harsh and lonely existence is softened by the gentle nursing of a young nun who serves others without thought of personal or material reward. 60 seconds.

Person to Person: Telespot from TeleKETICS.

A well-dressed woman on her way to church encounters several individuals of different ethnic backgrounds. With an air of superiority she enters the church to "worship" God, unaware that she has walked past him. 60 seconds.

The Puzzle: From TeleKETICS

A high-powered executive collides with a small "nobody" boy in a busy airport. His decision to come back and help gather the child's scattered puzzle pieces evokes the memorable question "Are you God?" 60 seconds.

The Stray: From TeleKETICS.

The familiar parable of the lost sheep takes on new dimensions in this story of thirteen first graders who spend a day at the zoo with a harried bus driver who is really a good shepherd at heart. When one of the children, "Tiger 12," strays from the "flock," viewers of all ages will not only share the child's anxiety in being separated from the group but will also experience the joyful celebration when he is found. 14 minutes.

Talent for Tony: From TeleKETICS.

The very human fear of making a mistake and being rejected is at the core of this modern version of the parable of the talents. When their artist father invites five-year-old Tony and his older brother and sister to create something for the upcoming art festival, Mike and Melinda quickly respond. Their drawings transport them into fantasy worlds beneath the sea and above the clouds. Tony is afraid to mar the white surface of his paper.

His fears take the form of a fierce lion. But through his father's concern, love, and acceptance, Tony discovers that the one talent to be treasured is belief in oneself. Recommended for primary age. 13 minutes.

William: From TeleKETICS.

William is a six-year-old who is too big to be a baby and too small to be "one of the guys." When his family participates in a community picnic, William tries to join in the fun but is ignored by everyone. Undaunted, he turns to his special sense of wonder that gives him "magic eyes" and is drawn into a world of hummingbirds and earthworms, dragonflies and rainbows. Eventually he emerges, following a snail's trail that leads him to a marvelous discovery. The whole community makes him a hero. Now William is special—or is it always special to be just William? 15 minutes.

Workout: From TeleKETICS.

Workout explores the relationship between a father and son who understand the same values in totally different ways. Unexpectedly visiting his son at college, the father is challenged to physical competition. Their workout quickly assumes symbolic proportions as father and son realize that conflicts between differing life views must themselves be encountered before encountering one another, and in turn, God. Senior high, adult. 15 minutes.

Filmstrips

The Magic Sampo: From TeleKETICS.

A Finnish folk tale centering around two brothers, one who works hard at his forge, the other, Darien, a dreamer. One day, the Snow Queen gives Darien the gift of song and the ability to make for her a magic sampo—a kind of cornucopia. But he can only make it if he works with his brother. The filmstrip can be an effective bridge to a discussion of sin as a failure to live up to one's potential. 55 frames, 8½ minutes.

The Wanderer: From TeleKETICS.

This creative exploration of the baptismal experience is a fable about a young man who sees the world "differently," in strange and unusual colors. He searches desperately for a community that will accept him and his vision—but everywhere he meets rejection and misunderstanding. Imaginative and rich in symbol, the filmstrip is ideal for young people seeking their own identity. 72 frames, 8 minutes.

Records

"Arch Books Aloud!" St. Louis, Mo.: Concordia Publishing House.

Records and storybooks of the following parables:

"The Good Samaritan," parable of love.

"The Boy Who Ran Away," prodigal son.

"Eight Bags of Gold," parable of the talents.

"Jon and the Little Lost Lamb," good shepherd.

"The House on the Rock," parable about foundations.

"The King's Invitation," parable of the marriage feast.

"The Unforgiving Servant," the forgiven man who forgave nothing.

"Two Men in the Temple," Pharisee and Publican.

"The Pearl That Changed a Life," parable of the pearl of great price.

"Sir Abner and His Grape Pickers," rich man and the vineyard.

"Free to Be You and Me." Marlo Thomas and Friends, Bell Records, 1972.

Contains stereo LP and twelve-page illustrated lyric booklet. Candid, humorous, tender, angry, and exuberant, these songs by Marlo Thomas and friends (Harry Belafonte, Mel Brooks, Jack Cassidy, Carol Channing, Tom Smothers, etc.) reflect what it means to be free of sexist stereotypes—to be you and me. Highly recommended for children of all ages—especially parents and teachers!

Habel, Norman C., *The Purple Puzzle Tree,* set number 5. St. Louis, Mo.: Concordia Publishing House.

"When Jesus Told His Parables " (the rich man and Lazarus and the prodigal son). The set includes six books and one 33 1/3 LP album with narration and background music. Other stories included in this album are: "The First True Super Star," "A Wild Young Man Called John," "The Dirty Devil and the Carpenter's Boy," "When Jesus Did His Miracles of Love," and "Old Rock the Fisherman."

Therese, Sister Miriam, "I Know the Secret." New York: Avant Garde Records.

Contains the original recordings of the songs in the book by the same name (see above under *Books for Singing*).

Miscellaneous Resources

Family Clustering, Inc., P. O. Box 18074, Rochester, NY 14618.

Write to this agency for more information regarding family cluster education.

Griggs, Donald L., *The Planning Game* (manual), 1971, Griggs Educational Service, 1731 Barcelona Street, Livermore, CA 94550.

A simulation game to assist teachers in lesson planning. Also, one of the card sets is on the parables ("Parables of Jesus") and lists several helpful resources and learning activities.

Koehler, George E., *Learning Together,* Discipleship Resources, P.O. Box 840, Nashville, TN 37202.

Appendix III.
Various Ways to Present Parables

There are several ways to present parables to add variety. Many different methods are suggested in this unit. Following is a list of methods and descriptions.

Banners: Banners, especially if made by families, provide a lasting memento of the session. Bright and varied colors of felt glued to burlap can be used to create symbols, words, phrases, or pictures that interpret the story. A good source for felt scraps is:

GAF Corporation
Hayward Street
Franklin, MA 02038

Specify size and colors when ordering. Minimum order is $10.00 (10 lbs.). Cost is $1.00 per pound plus $1.50 postage per 10 pounds. These prices are subject to change. (See Session III.)

Creative Writing: Almost anyone can retell a parable in his or her words. But one has to understand its main point quite well before one can paraphrase it. Creative writing can take several forms, including poetry, prose, skits, and litanies. (See Sessions I and V.)

Collages: Making collages is simple, fun, and helps to get rid of old papers and magazines by recycling them. Pictures or headlines are cut out of magazines or newspapers and arranged on a large piece of butcher paper or newsprint in a way that interprets the meaning of the parable. (See Sessions I and IV.)

Dramatizations: Simply have characters, dressed up in makeshift costumes, reenact the parable as it is written. A group can be asked to prepare ahead of time, or the preparation can be the primary activity of the session, having several groups recreate the parable for the other participants.

Drawing and Coloring Pictures: Any child, from age four to eighty, can draw and color pictures of what he or she "sees" in a parable or story. It's a great way to help the adults and children communicate with each other as they talk about their pictures. (See Session VI.)

Field Trips: Visiting places and people who work with needs that are reflected in the parable is a good way to gain an understanding of the modern application of the story. (See Session IV.)

Finger Painting: This is a fun way to express emotion and feelings on paper and have the same fun you had as a child making mud pies. Colors and designs that reflect the feelings the person senses in the story or parable are created on butcher paper. The easiest way to make finger paints is to pour enough liquid laundry starch on a piece of butcher paper to cover it, then sprinkle the desired color of tempera paint on the starch. The student can then spread it around the paper to make designs. (See Session II.)

Fishbowl Role Play: The leader provides descriptions as in regular role play, but each participant has a small group from whom he or she receives suggestions on how to play the role. (See Session III.)

Puppets: Children usually find it easier to act through puppets than to be directly involved. They can be used in dramatization, role play, skits, or even storytelling. Create them from paper sacks or from old socks. Make them in advance or as a lesson activity. Puppets are not specifically suggested in any of the sessions of this unit. However, they could be used any time that a skit, role play, or dramatization is suggested.

Role Play: Give the participants brief descriptions of the roles they are to play and let them develop their own plot as they participate in the role play. Role play works best if the roles and situations are modern. (See Sessions II and IV.)

Skits: This is another way to dramatize a parable, either in its original form or in a modern setting. The characters may prepare their own skit in advance, act impromptu, or they may use one that is already prepared in the material or by the leader. Costuming is optional. (See Sessions I, II, III, and V.)

Simulation Games: The idea of simulation games is to recreate a modern experience that deals with the same topic as the parable. It may involve all the class members. Role play is a type of simulation, though not quite as involved as most simulation games. You can create your own or use some that already exist. (See Session IV.)

Storytelling: The parables may be retold in modern language. Modern stories that deal with the same topic may also be used. They should be stories that call to mind pictures of concrete situations rather than abstract ideas. (See Sessions V and VI.)

Bibliography

Barclay, William, *The Gospel of Luke.* Philadelphia: The Westminster Press, 1956.

—————, *The Gospel of Matthew,* vol. 2. Philadelphia: The Westminster Press, 1958.

Christine, Charles T. and Dorothy W., *Practical Guide to Curriculum and Instruction.* Englewood Cliffs, N.J.: Prentice-Hall, Inc., 1971.

Mager, Robert F., *Preparing Instructional Objectives.* Belmont, Calif.: Fearon Publishers, Inc., 1962.

Rozeboom, John D., *Family Camping—Five Designs for Your Church.* Nashville: Board of Discipleship of the United Methodist Church, 1973.